IWCS Workshop on Foundations of Situated and Multimodal Communication 2017

Montpellier, France
19 – 22 September 2017

ISBN: 978-1-5108-5284-6

Printed from e-media with permission by:

Curran Associates, Inc.
57 Morehouse Lane
Red Hook, NY 12571

Some format issues inherent in the e-media version may also appear in this print version.

Printed by Curran Associates, Inc. (2017)

For permission requests, please contact the Association for Computational Linguistics at the address below.

Association for Computational Linguistics
209 N. Eighth Street
Stroudsburg, Pennsylvania 18360

Phone: 1-570-476-8006
Fax: 1-570-476-0860

acl@aclweb.org

Additional copies of this publication are available from:

Curran Associates, Inc.
57 Morehouse Lane
Red Hook, NY 12571 USA
Phone: 845-758-0400
Fax: 845-758-2633
Email: curran@proceedings.com
Web: www.proceedings.com

TABLE OF CONTENTS

Proceedings of the IWCS Workshop *Foundations of Situated and Multimodal Communication*

Workshop organizers: Nicholas Asher, Julie Hunter, Alex Lascarides

Situated or multimodal communication, in which speakers exploit various aspects of the nonlinguistic context to communicate a message, is a fact of life for face-to-face conversations. Its analysis is of fundamental importance to modelling everyday conversations between humans and embodied conversations between humans and robots. However, the approach in formal semantics to the study of how nonlinguistic and linguistic contexts interact has not evolved dramatically since Kaplan's seminal work on indexicals and demonstratives. The goal of this workshop was to bring together both linguists and computer scientists to discuss foundational, conceptual, and practical issues involving situated communication.

Invited Talks:

Cynthia Matuszek, "Grounded Language Acquisition: A Physical Agent Approach"

Siddharth Narayanaswamy, "Language- and Model-Driven Machine Intelligence"

Contributed Talks:

Sai Abishek Bhaskar, Maximillian Kper, Sabine Schulte Im Walde, & Diego Frassinelli, "Exploring Multi-Modal Text+Image Models to Distinguish between Abstract and Concrete Nouns"

Andy Lcking, "Indexicals as Weak Descriptors"

James Pustejovsky, Nikhil Krishnaswamy, Bruce Draper, Pradyumna Narayana, Rahul Bangar,"Creating Common Ground through Multimodal Simulations"

Ielka van der Sluis, Anne Nienke Eppinga, Gisela Redeker, "Text-Picture Relations in Multimodal Instructions"

Program Committee:

Ellen Breitholtz
Sam Carter
Tim van der Cruys
Simon Dobnik
Christine Howes
Jonathan Ginzburg
Manuel Giuliani
Jeremy Kuhn
Andy Lcking
Cynthia Matuszek
Siddharth Narayanaswamy
David Schlangen
Matthew Stone
Luke Zettlemoyer

Exploring Multi-Modal Text+Image Models to Distinguish between Abstract and Concrete Nouns

Sai Abishek Bhaskar
Manipal Institute of Technology, India
sai.abishek@learner.manipal.edu

Maximilian Köper, Sabine Schulte Im Walde and Diego Frassinelli
University of Stuttgart, Germany
{koepermn,schulte,frassinelli}@ims.uni-stuttgart.de

Abstract

This paper explores variants of multi-modal computational models that aim to distinguish between abstract and concrete nouns. We assumed that textual vs. visual modalities might have different strengths in providing information on abstract vs. concrete words. While the overall predictions of our models were highly successful (reaching an accuracy of 96.45% in a binary classification and a Spearman correlation of 0.86 in a regression analysis), the differences between the textual, visual and combined modalities were however negligible, hence both text and images seem to provide reliable, non-complementary information to represent both abstract and concrete words.

1 Introduction

Over the years, different disciplines have been interested in exploring the contributions of contextual and perceptual information in human language acquisition and processing. From a psycholinguistic perspective, the grounding theory indicates that the mental representation of a concept is built not only through linguistic exposure but also incorporating multi-modal information extracted from real world situations, including auditory, visual, etc. stimuli (Barsalou, 1999; Shapiro, 2007; Glenberg and Kaschak, 2002). From a computational perspective, multi-modality has been shown to enhance corpus-based co-occurrence models that predict lexical information on various tasks, such as simulating word association, predicting semantic and visual similarity, determining the compositionality of multi-word expressions, and distinguishing between abstract and concrete concepts (Andrews et al., 2008; Silberer and Lapata, 2012; Roller and Schulte im Walde, 2013; Bruni et al., 2014; Hill et al., 2014; Lazaridou et al., 2015).

One focus of interest on the computational side has addressed the question of when and which perceptual information is helpful for semantic predictions in computational models, i.e., under which conditions perceptual information enhances or even outperforms textual information. For example, previous work described filters that added visual information to corpus-based information into a computational model of word meaning only in specific conditions: Kiela et al. (2014) suggested the *dispersion filter* that integrates only images that resemble each other to a certain degree. Köper and Schulte im Walde (2017) applied the same filter to a computational model of compositionality and added two more filters: the *imageability filter* integrating only images for highly imaginable words, as determined by existing imageability ratings; and the *clustering filter* only using images for a word that were similar to each other, as determined by a cluster analysis.

In this paper, we explore variants of multi-modal computational models that aim to distinguish between abstract and concrete nouns, to contribute to both psycholinguistic research by exploring differences in abstract vs. concrete concept representation and processing (Murphy, 2002; Barsalou and Wiemer-Hastings, 2005; Pecher et al., 2011), and to computational linguistic research by exploring differences between textual and visual information in modelling semantic knowledge. More specifically, we apply a binary classifier as well as a regression model to differentiate between abstract vs. concrete English nouns, as determined by concreteness ratings from Brysbaert et al. (2014). As features we compare standard textual count co-occurrences from a web corpus (Schäfer and Bildhauer, 2012), *word2vec* embeddings (Mikolov et al., 2013), *GoogLeNet* image vectors (Szegedy et al., 2015), and variants of text and image vector concatenation. As qualitative analysis, we compare classification errors across modalities, to zoom into the strengths and limits of the modalities and model parameters.

2 Material and Methods

2.1 Target Words

For our studies, we extracted nouns from the Brysbaert et al. (2014) collection of concreteness ratings for 40,000 English words. In this collection, each word was evaluated by at least 25 participants on a scale from 1 (abstract) to 5 (concrete). Given that participants were not aware of the part-of-speech (POS) of the word they were rating, we automatically assigned each word its most frequently occurring POS in our corpus (see Section 2.2). We focused our analyses on nouns because they are usually easier for humans to classify according to their concreteness compared to adjectives and verbs. In total we had 9,241 nouns that were also covered in an extensive selection of behavioural measures, such as valency scores (Warriner et al., 2013) and reaction times (Balota et al., 2007), which we aim to include in further analyses.

In one of our classification experiments (see Section 2.3), we included only a subset of the 9,241 nouns, i.e., the 1,000 most abstract and the 1,000 most concrete nouns, in order to assess a binary distinction of the most extreme noun instances regarding their abstractness vs. concreteness.

Figure 1 shows the distribution of the abstractness/concreteness scores across the 9,241 target nouns in two different ways. In the upper plot, the histogram indicates that there are considerably more concrete than abstract target nouns, which is the reason why we did not select nouns from specific ranges (e.g., 1–2 for abstract nouns vs. 4–5 for concrete nouns) for the binary classification, but rather an identical number of nouns from the two extremes (i.e., 1,000 nouns from the extreme ranges of each category). In the lower plot, the boxplots show the quartiles for the two sets of selected abstract/concrete targets vs. the remaining "middle" set of 7,241 nouns. This view once more illustrates that the 1,000 most abstract nouns cover a larger range of scores (from 1.07 for *spirituality* to 2.17 for *skill*) than the 1,000 most concrete nouns (from 4.97 for e.g. *shoe* to 5.00 for e.g. *lemon*), and also that the median of the middle part is rather high (i.e., confirming that many targets are highly concrete).

2.2 Text and Image Data

As textual modality for our target nouns, we compared standard count co-occurrence vectors and *word2vec* embedding vectors. The count vectors used *ENCOW14* (Schäfer and Bildhauer, 2012; Schäfer, 2015), currently one of the largest web corpora, to induce co-occurrence frequency matrices for the target nouns. As dimensions in the target noun vectors we compared two variants: on the one hand, we used the full set of 9,241 target nouns as co-occurring word dimensions; on the other hand, we used the reduced set of 2,000 target nouns as co-occurring word dimensions. The main reason for using the targets also as vector dimensions was to enable explorations of interdependencies between the abstractness/concreteness scores of our targets and their co-occurring words (see Frassinelli et al. (2017) for details). As window size for the co-occurrence counts we looked at two words to the left and to the right of the target words. As embedding vectors, we used the publicly available representations obtained from the *word2vec* cbow model (Mikolov et al., 2013). This model was trained on a Google-internal news corpus with 100 billion tokens.

The visual features were extracted from images downloaded from the Google search engine, following Kiela et al. (2016). We queried the search engine for up to 25 images per word, and converted all images into high-dimensional numerical representations by using the *Caffe* toolkit (Jia et al., 2014) and pre-trained models.

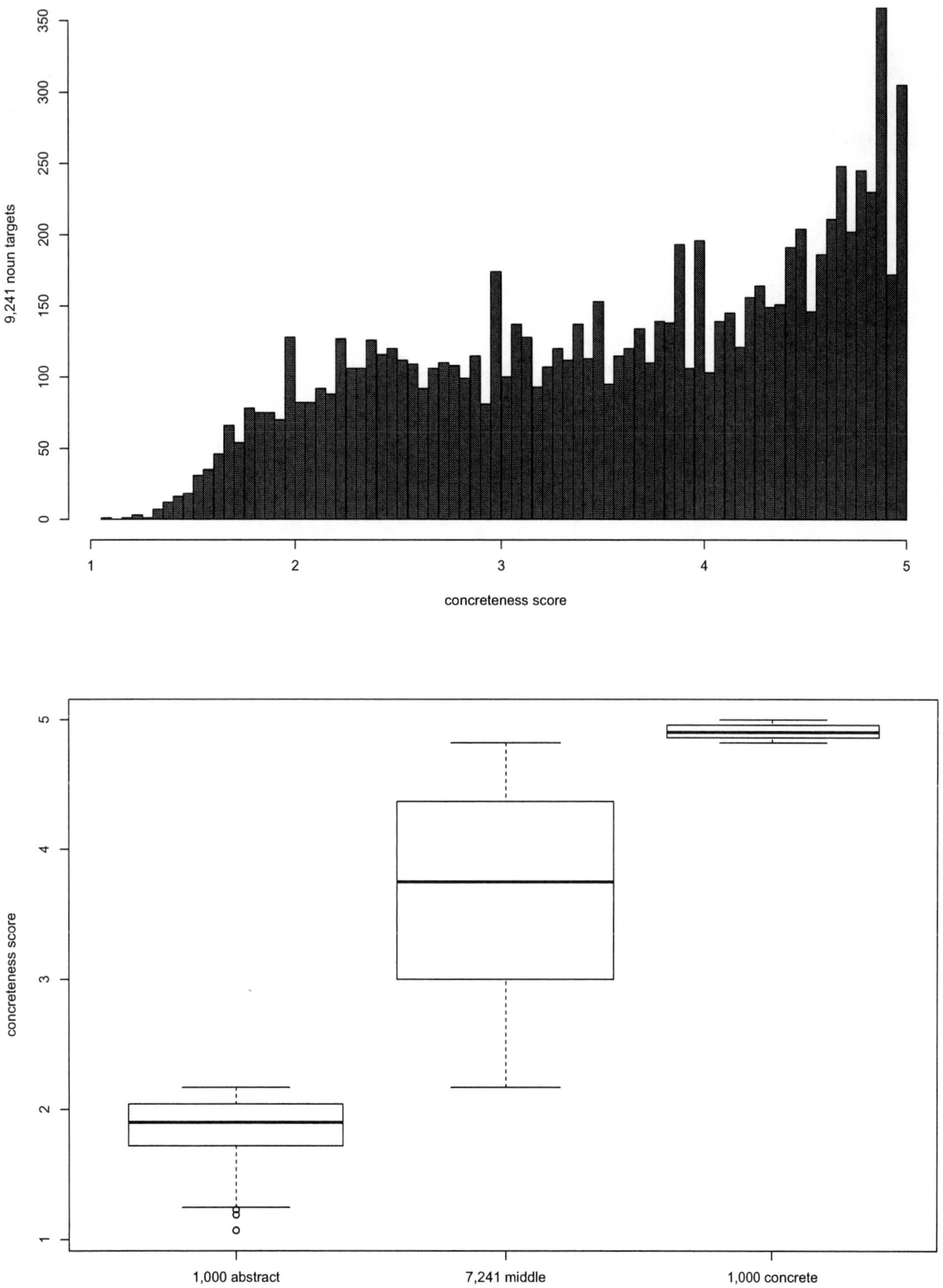

Figure 1: Abstractness/concreteness scores across our 9,241 target nouns.

For image recognition, we applied state-of-the-art convolutional neural networks:

1. BVLC *GoogLeNet* (Szegedy et al., 2015), a 22-layer deep network. We obtained vectors by outputting the value of layer pool5/7x7 s1, which is the last layer before the final softmax and contains 1,024 elements. These 1,024 elements determine the dimensionality of our vectors.

2. BVLC *AlexNet* (Krizhevsky et al., 2012), a neural network with 60 million parameters and 500,000 neurons, consisting of five convolutional layers, some of which are followed by max-pooling layers, and two globally connected layers with a final 1,000-way softmax. We output the vectors from layer fc7, a 4,096-dimensional feature vector for every image.

In all settings, a word is represented in the visual space by the mean vector of its (up to) 25 image representations.

When concatenating the textual and visual target vectors, we compared two variants:

1. CONCAT-SIMPLE: We concatenated the two vectors for each target noun without normalisation, i.e., disregarding the different dimensionalities of the vectors.

2. CONCAT-NORM: We concatenated the two vectors for each target noun after normalisation, i.e., we first calculated the proportion of each dimension in the two vectors separately, before concatenating them.

2.3 Classification

In order to evaluate the performance of our models in correctly classifying words according to their concreteness scores, we performed 10-fold cross-validation on the output of two classification tasks.

1. BINARY CLASSIFICATION: A binary classification of the most extreme abstract vs. concrete nouns should offer the best access to the relevance of the different modalities. This classification thus makes use of the subset of 2,000 target nouns (1,000 extremely abstract and 1,000 extremely concrete nouns), and applies a Random Forest Classifier. The binary classification is evaluated by computing the accuracy of the class assignments.

2. REGRESSION MODEL: In the second classification setup, we apply Gradient Boosting to predict the abstractness/concreteness scores for all 9,241 target nouns, for the subset of 2,000 target nouns, and for the "middle" set of 7,241 target nouns. The predicted scores are evaluated against the human ratings from the Brysbaert et al. (2014) collection using Spearman's rank-order correlation coefficient ρ.

3 Results

In this section, we present the classification and regression results of our experiments, across the various sets of target nouns, their textual and visual features, and the two classification methods.

3.1 Quantitative Results

Table 1 shows a quantitative view on the results. For the binary classification, we compare the textual and visual features for the 2,000 extreme abstract/concrete target nouns. For the regression model, we compare the same features for the full set of 9,241 target nouns, the 2,000 extreme target nouns, as well as the "middle" set. Since there were only marginal differences between using 2,000 vs. 9,241 count vector dimensions as well as between using AlexNet vs. GoogLeNet image vectors, we selected only one from each of the alternatives for presentation. Regarding the concatenation of the vectors, the normalised version CONCAT-NORM consistently outperformed the non-normalised concatenation, so we focus on the former.

Targets	Text (T) 9241 (count)	Text (T) word2vec	Images (V) GoogLeNet	Text+Images (T+V) 2000+GoogLeNet	Text+Images (T+V) 9241+GoogLeNet	Text+Images (T+V) word2vec+GoogLeNet
Binary Classification *(evaluation: accuracy)*						
2,000	94.78	92.21	92.79	95.89	**96.45**	93.79
Regression Model *(evaluation: ρ)*						
2,000	**0.78**	0.77	0.75	0.77	**0.78**	0.77
7,241	0.75	0.73	0.61	0.76	**0.79**	0.76
9,241	0.83	0.82	0.71	0.84	**0.86**	0.83

Table 1: Classification and regression results.

The differences between the textual (T), the visual (V) and the concatenated textual+visual (T+V) features are marginal. Looking at the best results per category (T/V/T+V), the textual features are slightly better than the visual features in the binary distinction between extremely abstract vs. concrete target nouns, and the combined multi-modal features are slightly better than the text-only features. For both the textual mode and the multi-modal mode, the count vectors slightly outperform the embedding vectors.

The same tendencies can be observed in the regression model, though the difference between the count and embedding vectors vanishes, and the differences between the modalities differ across the target noun sets: the predicted rankings of the concreteness scores have a better fit to the human rankings when taking all 9,241 target nouns into account, in comparison to taking subsets into account. In addition, the difference between relying on textual vs. visual information is stronger for the larger sets of 7,241 and 9,241 target nouns than for the set of 2,000 nouns.

3.2 Qualitative Results

The quantitative analysis showed that the improvements in semantic classification when using images in addition to text information were only marginal. We therefore aimed to explore differences in our abstractness/concreteness classifications across modalities by relying on a qualitative analysis.

Table 2 shows the strongest differences in abstractness/concreteness binary classification when comparing the best textual model (9241 count) and the best visual model (GoogLeNet), by calculating the disagreements between predictions and human ratings. I.e., the column 'T > V' lists the 15 target nouns where the error between prediction and gold standard was much smaller across the many runs when relying on the textual vs. the visual features; vice versa for the column 'T < V'. We can see that –according to our small sample– none of the differences in classification can clearly be attributed to only abstract (see 'A' and magenta font) or only concrete (see 'C' and blue font) target nouns: 7 out of the top 15 words that are classified better when relying on textual rather than visual features are concrete, as are 9 out of the top 15 words that are classified better when relying on visual rather than textual features. More or less the same applies in Table 3 when comparing the textual and the textual+visual features (9 out of 15 words for T vs. 7 out of 15 words for T+V are concrete).

4 Conclusion

In this paper, we explored variants of multi-modal computational models that aimed to distinguish between abstract and concrete nouns. While the overall predictions of many variants were highly successful (reaching an accuracy of 96.45% in a binary classification and a Spearman correlation of 0.86 using a regression model), the differences between the textual, visual and combined modalities were negligible, hence the information types in the different modalities are not complementary. A small-scale qualitative evaluation indicated that all variants of modalities do model both abstract and concrete words similarly well, i.e., both text and images seem to provide sufficient information to represent both abstract and concrete words.

T > V			**T < V**		
Target	Score	Abstract/Concrete	Target	Score	Abstract/Concrete
trickery	1.90	A	sausage	4.88	C
bamboo	4.86	C	butter	4.90	C
satire	1.96	A	firewood	4.93	C
bull	4.85	C	snout	4.89	C
extravagance	1.73	A	willingness	1.81	A
lightbulb	5.00	C	underpants	4.89	C
marshmallow	4.85	C	sociology	1.79	A
whim	1.69	A	gutter	4.85	C
regression	1.92	A	reason	1.93	A
thanks	2.15	A	bone	4.90	C
oven	4.97	C	purpose	1.52	A
pitcher	4.93	C	frustration	2.06	A
sentimentality	1.73	A	sparrow	4.85	C
bandage	4.85	C	cowardice	2.10	A
dishonesty	1.90	A	thought	1.97	C

Table 2: Most striking classification differences using textual vs. visual features.

T > T+V			**T < T+V**		
Target	Score	Abstract/Concrete	Target	Score	Abstract/Concrete
beard	4.96	C	principle	1.70	A
offensive	2.10	A	sausage	4.88	C
severity	1.76	A	purpose	1.52	A
ecstasy	2.04	A	reason	1.93	A
bowl	4.87	C	butter	4.99	C
lollipop	4.96	C	impossibility	1.52	A
walnut	4.97	C	sociology	1.79	A
breakup	2.00	A	underpants	4.89	C
fridge	4.92	C	willingness	1.81	A
complement	2.00	A	bone	4.90	C
hotel	4.93	C	gutter	4.85	C
butterfly	4.93	C	firewood	4.93	C
wish	1.77	A	frustration	2.06	A
jeans	5.00	C	weird	1.59	A
cabin	4.92	C	snout	4.89	C

Table 3: Most striking classification differences using textual vs. textual+visual features.

Acknowledgments

The first author (Sai Abishek Bhaskar) would like to thank his parents for supporting him during his time at the University of Stuttgart. The research was further supported by the DFG Collaborative Research Centre SFB 732 (Diego Frassinelli, Maximilian Köper), and the DFG Heisenberg Fellowship SCHU-2580/1 (Sabine Schulte im Walde). We also thank the two anonymous reviewers for their comments.

References

Mark Andrews, David Vinson, and Gabriella Vigliocco. Inferring a Probabilistic Model of Semantic Memory from Word Association Norms. In *Proceedings of the 30th Annual Conference of the Cognitive Science Society*, 2008.

David A. Balota, Melvin J. Yap, Michael J. Cortese, Keith A. Hutchison, Brett Kessler, Bjorn Loftis, James H. Neely, Douglas L. Nelson, Greg B. Simpson, and Rebecca Treiman. The English Lexicon Project. *Behavior Research Methods*, 39(3):445–459, 2007.

Lawrence W. Barsalou. Perceptual Symbol Systems. *Behavioral and Brain Sciences*, 22:577–660, 1999.

Lawrence W. Barsalou and Katja Wiemer-Hastings. Situating Abstract Concepts. In D. Pecher and R. Zwaan, editors, *Grounding cognition: The role of perception and action in memory, language, and thinking*, chapter 7, pages 129–163. Cambridge University Press, New York, 2005.

Elia Bruni, Nam-Khanh Tran, and Marco Baroni. Multimodal Distributional Semantics. *Journal of Artificial Intelligence Research*, 49:1–47, 2014.

Marc Brysbaert, Amy Beth Warriner, and Victor Kuperman. Concreteness Ratings for 40 Thousand generally known English Word Lemmas. *Behavior Research Methods*, 64:904–911, 2014.

Diego Frassinelli, Daniela Naumann, Jason Utt, and Sabine Schulte im Walde. Contextual Characteristics of Concrete and Abstract Words. In *Proceedings of the 12th International Conference on Computational Semantics*, Montpellier, France, 2017. To appear.

Arthur M. Glenberg and Michael P. Kaschak. Grounding Language in Action. *Psychonomic Bulletin and Review*, 9(3):558–565, 2002.

Felix Hill, Roi Reichart, and Anna Korhonen. Multi-Modal Models for Concrete and Abstract Concept Meaning. *Transactions of the Association for Computational Linguistics*, 2(1):285–296, 2014.

Yangqing Jia, Evan Shelhamer, Jeff Donahue, Sergey Karayev, Jonathan Long, Ross Girshick, Sergio Guadarrama, and Trevor Darrell. Caffe: Convolutional Architecture for Fast Feature Embedding. *arXiv preprint arXiv:1408.5093*, 2014.

Douwe Kiela, Felix Hill, Anna Korhonen, and Stephen Clark. Improving Multi-Modal Representations Using Image Dispersion: Why Less is Sometimes More. In *Proceedings of the 52nd Annual Meeting of the Association for Computational Linguistics*, pages 835–841, 2014.

Douwe Kiela, Anita L. Verő, and Stephen Clark. Comparing Data Sources and Architectures for Deep Visual Representation Learning in Semantics. In *Proceedings of the Conference on Empirical Methods in Natural Language Processing*, 2016.

Maximilian Köper and Sabine Schulte im Walde. Complex Verbs are Different: Exploring the Visual Modality in Multi-Modal Models to Predict Compositionality. In *Proceedings of the 13th Workshop on Multiword Expressions*, pages 200–206, Valencia, Spain, 2017.

Alex Krizhevsky, Ilya Sutskever, and Geoffrey E. Hinton. ImageNet Classification with Deep Convolutional Neural Networks. In F. Pereira, C. J. C. Burges, L. Bottou, and K. Q. Weinberger, editors, *Advances in Neural Information Processing Systems 25*, pages 1097–1105. 2012.

Angeliki Lazaridou, Nghia The Pham, and Marco Baroni. Combining Language and Vision with a Multimodal Skip-gram Model. In *Proceedings of the Conference of the North American Chapter of the Association for Computational Linguistics: Human Language Technologies*, pages 153–163, Denver, Colorado, 2015.

Tomas Mikolov, Ilya Sutskever, Kai Chen, Greg S. Corrado, and Jeff Dean. Distributed Representations of Words and Phrases and their Compositionality. In *Advances in Neural Information Processing Systems 26*, pages 3111–3119, Lake Tahoe, Nevada, USA, 2013.

Gregory Murphy. *The Big Book of Concepts*. MIT Press, 2002.

Diane Pecher, Inge Boot, and Saskia Van Dantzig. Abstract Concepts. Sensory-Motor Grounding, Metaphors, and Beyond. *Psychology of Learning and Motivation – Advances in Research and Theory*, 54:217–248, 2011.

Stephen Roller and Sabine Schulte im Walde. A Multimodal LDA Model integrating Textual, Cognitive and Visual Modalities. In *Proceedings of the Conference on Empirical Methods in Natural Language Processing*, pages 1146–1157, Seattle, WA, 2013.

Roland Schäfer. Processing and Querying Large Web Corpora with the COW14 Architecture. In *Proceedings of the 3rd Workshop on Challenges in the Management of Large Corpora*, pages 28–34, Mannheim, Germany, 2015.

Roland Schäfer and Felix Bildhauer. Building Large Corpora from the Web Using a New Efficient Tool Chain. In *Proceedings of the 8th International Conference on Language Resources and Evaluation*, pages 486–493, Istanbul, Turkey, 2012.

Larry Shapiro. The Embodied Cognition Research Programme. *Philosophy Compass*, 2(2):338–346, 2007.

Carina Silberer and Mirella Lapata. Grounded Models of Semantic Representation. In *Proceedings of the Joint Conference on Empirical Methods in Natural Language Processing and Computational Natural Language Learning*, pages 1423–1433, Jeju Island, Korea, 2012.

Christian Szegedy, Wei Liu, Yangqing Jia, Pierre Sermanet, Scott Reed, Dragomir Anguelov, Dumitru Erhan, Vincent Vanhoucke, and Andrew Rabinovich. Going Deeper with Convolutions. *Computer Vision and Pattern Recognition*, 2015.

Amy Beth Warriner, Victor Kuperman, and Marc Brysbaert. Norms of Valence, Arousal, and Dominance for 13,915 English Lemmas. *Behavior Research Methods*, 45(4):1191–1207, 2013.

Indexicals as Weak Descriptors

Andy Lücking
Goethe University Frankfurt

Abstract

Indexicals have a couple of uses that are in conflict with the traditional view that they directly refer to indices in the utterance situation. But how do they refer instead? It is argued that indexicals have both an indexical and a descriptive aspect – why they are called *weak descriptors* here. The indexical aspect anchors them in the actual situation of utterance, the weak descriptive aspect singles out the referent. Descriptive uses of "today" are then attributed to calendric coercion which is triggered by qunatificational elements. This account provides a grammatically motivated formal link to descriptive uses. With regard to some uses of "I", a tentative contiguity rule is proposed as the reference rule for the first person pronoun, which is oriented along recent hearer-oriented accounts in philosophy, but finally has to be criticized.

1 Descriptive Indexicals

Indexicals have descriptive uses as exemplified in (1a) (taken from Nunberg, 2004, p. 265):

(1) a. Today is always the biggest party day of the year.
  b. *November 1, 2000 is always the biggest party day of the year.

According to Nunberg (2004), *today* in (1a) is interpreted as picking out a day type or day property instead of referring to a concrete day, since "[...] the interpretations of these uses of indexicals are the very things that their linguistic meanings pick out of the context." (p. 272). The full date in (1b), to the contrary, refers to a particular day and has no such type or property reading. The interpretations of both sentences in (1) diverge, even if both sentences are produced on November 1, 2000. Based on these observations (and criticizing his earlier account which rests on distinguishing the index from the referent and bridging between both by means of a salient relation (Nunberg, 1993)) Nunberg (2004) comes up with his *granularization of context hypothesis*: indexical expressions are evaluated in contexts which are "individuated by the conversationally relevant properties" (p. 273). However, the "conversationally relevant properties" seem to be restricted by the linguistic meaning of the indexical in question. For instance, descriptive uses of *today* always rest on a temporal interpretation (combining *today* with atemporal descriptions sound awkward, e.g., "*Today is always $2+2=4$" or "*Today is always the largest tree in the park"). Thus, a more restrictive account should be possible.

Accordingly, contrary to the context granularization account – at least with respect to the kinds of examples in (1) – it is argued in the following, that descriptive interpretations of indexical expressions are functional abstractions over indices that follow from the grammar of descriptive constructions in addition to type raising (Section 2). Part of the argument is that indexicals have a weak descriptive content that allows for functional abstraction in the first place. This re-analysis is spelled out more precisely in Section 3. Contrary to this line, however, in Section 4 it is suggested that 'I', instead of exhibiting descriptive use, should be interpreted according to a addressee-oriented semantic rule resting on a contiguity relation.

2 "Today" and Calendric Coercion

The standard interpretation of descriptive indexicals rests on the two stage process of deferred reference: first, the index is identified and then the referent is found via a salient functional relation it bears to the index (Nunberg, 1993; Elbourne, 2008). Why looking for another analysis? A reason is that descriptive readings can be obtained with exophorically used demonstratives, but not with their endophoric counterparts (cf. Nunberg, 2004, p. 271):

(2) a. [Pointing at Pope Francis] That man is usually Italian.

b. *I met Pope Francis yesterday. That man is usually Italian.

The problem then is, why the salient relation bound up with the index is functional in one case, but non-functional in the other.

Further evidence for this mismatch can be found when comparing descriptive uses of indexicals to E-type pronouns (Dowty, 1981), respectively and more specifically, the "paycheck" readings of implicit arguments as analysed by Pedersen (2011).[1] The "paycheck" pronoun in (3a) (bold face, my emphasis – both sentences in (3) are taken from Pedersen (2011, p. 159), where (3a) is a variant of the original sentence provided by Dowty (1981).) receives a functional reading on top of an anaphoric one to the effect that *it* refers to the paycheck of the foolish man instead to that of the wise man (the simple anaphoric interpretation).

(3) a. The wise man gave his paycheck to his wife. The foolish man gave **it** to his mistress.

b. Every good father visits his daughter on her birthday. Bill's a deadbeat dad, so he only calls __.

The pronoun is analysed as an E-type pronoun in that it picks up a "paycheck-of" function from the preceding co-text and applies it to the variable index of its antecedent expression (*foolish man*, in this case). Accordingly, such E-type readings can be modelled as NP-deletion (Elbourne, 2001), giving rise to a formal link. Also implicit arguments can "hide" paycheck pronouns, as illustrated in (4b). The elliptic constituent, indicated by '__', when explicated spells out as "**his** daughter" and contains a paycheck possessive.

Implicit arguments bear the risk of overgeneralization, as has been argued by Heim (1990, p. 165). E-type accounts need to distinguish between (4a), which allows an E-type reading of *her*, from (4a), which, although conveying the same information, only allows a referential interpretation of *her*:

(4) a. Every man who has a wife is sitting next to her.

b. ?Every married man is sitting next to her.

Seen from the perspective of E-type pronouns, some challenges imposed specifically by descriptive uses of indexicals can be highlighted.

1. Descriptive indexicals lack a linguistic co-text from which a descriptive conditions can be taken. The running example of *today* given in (1a) is a case in point as is the demonstrative in (2a).

2. Even if their is a linguistic co-text, descriptive indexicals involve a deferred component that goes beyond the description taken from co-text. Consider (2) from above. The antecedent expression is a proper name, but what is required in order to account for the interpretation in question is a transition from the namebearer to its office or periods of papal reign. For such reasons, formal links like NP-deletion are not sufficient but deferred reference analyses are employed that draw on salient relations that are at their disposal just as required (see e.g. Elbourne, 2008).

[1] Accounting for descriptive indexicals in terms of a paycheck analysis is due to a suggestion of an anonymous reviewer.

3. A deferred reference analysis as sketched in the preceding bullet point surely accounts for descriptive indexicals. But then it has to face the non-transferrability of the deferring salient relation to discourse deixis, as exemplified in (2).

It seems that there lures an impasse in any modeling choice we can take along the E-type lines, in addition to a lack of explanation for the salient deferring relations just being there on demand.[2] However, the phenomenon of descriptive indexicals seem to be describable in more detailed terms.

First of all, more linguistic features that seem to be involved in licensing descriptive uses of indexicals can be identified. The descriptive interpretation in (4a) cannot simply be reduced to a certain *use* of the indexical: it is triggered by applying an adverbial quantifier (A-quantifier) to the indexical in the first place (Kijania-Placek, 2015). This is evidenced by the fact that no descriptive interpretation is available when the A-quantifier is absent (which also results in a specific interpretation of the definite):

(5) a. Today is the biggest party day of the year.

b. November 1, 2000 is the biggest party day of the year.

The same diagnosis applies to further examples which are discussed in this context, like those in (6). Again, the descriptive reading is linked to an A-quantifier – if the A-quantifier is absent, only a referential interpretation is available.

(6) a. [*Pointing at the pope*] He is (usually) Italian.

b. [*Watching Bayern against BVB*] This football match is (commonly) exciting.

When an A-quantifier is present, the meaning of the indexical is shifted from a referent to, for instance, its office (6b) or kind (6c).

Other quantifying contexts also give rise to descriptive readings:[3]

(7) a. Today is may favourite day.

b. Over the years, most couples request today as their marrying day.

(The quantifying aspect of adjective *favourite* may reside in introducing a comparison set.) Thus, it seems to be promising to ascribe the source for a shifted interpretation of descriptive indexicals to some sort of quantification.

Note further that the classic examples for descriptive readings of indexical expressions involve a form of the lexeme *be* followed by a predicational noun phrase (an exception being the more laborious construction in (7), though). As testified in (8), descriptive interpretations become unavailable when predicational constructions are replaced by regular verb phrases.[4]

(8) a. He usually visits an Italian.

b. This match commonly excites people.

In (8a), some custom behavior is ascribed to a referent. In a similar manner, a certain match is said to have a broad impact in (8b).[5]

Thus, the phenomenon of descriptive indexicals usually is invoked by

- predication over an indexical subject, where

[2]Note that the nature of the formal link between linguistic co-text and anaphoric indirect arguments is also recognized by Pedersen (2011) as one of the crucial challenges of any approach resting on additional, contextual functions.

[3]This observation and respective examples are contributed by the anonymous reviewers.

[4]Interestingly, as noted by an anonymous reviewer, this grammatical change is bound up with a switching from an individual-level to a stage-level predicate. This observation might shed some light on the sensitivity of descriptive indexicals to quantificational contexts.

[5]Many if not all demonstrative noun phrases have kind reading, anyway (Umbach and Gust, 2014), so that (8b) is ambiguous.

- the grammatical realization of the predication involves a *be* equation, and
- the predication is quantified.

In generalized quantifier theory, A-quantifiers can be interpreted in terms of determiner quantifiers (D-quantifiers; see e.g. Keenan, 2011). For instance, *always* corresponds to the universal quantifier *all*, which expresses a subset relation between sets X and Y, such that $\mathbf{all}(X)(Y)$ is true just in case $X \subseteq Y$. However, since *today* is an indexical expression, it does not give rise to a set denotation as required in (8). Using a contextual relation f as in works on deferred reference, the indexical can be type-raised by abstracting over the index.[6] The sentence in (1a) can now be roughly represented as follows:

(9) $\lambda f_{\langle e,e\rangle}[\{y : f(y) \wedge \mathbf{today}(y)\} \subseteq \{\mathbf{biggest\text{-}party\text{-}day\text{-}of\text{-}year}(y)\}]$

The idea of the semantic representation in (9) is to request a function f that maps its variable y onto years. The indexical *today* is then applied to this year.

The type mismatch arising due to quantificational co-texts seem to provide a suitable explanations for applying a re-interpretation of indexicals. In the following, a coercion model for such an operation is sketched. The strategy is as follows:

- The indexical picks out an individual but is descriptively underspecific (that is, the referent is not (only) singled out by descriptive means).
- The descriptive underspecificity allows for a contextual abstraction over the referent, where the dimension of abstraction is determined by the quantifier.

The framework for providing a more precise spell-out is the dialogue theory *KoS* (Ginzburg, 2012) implemented in *Type Theory with Records* (Cooper, 2012; Cooper and Ginzburg, 2015). KoS provides an interface to context, which is required for situated language means like indexicals.

3 Abstraction over Contextual Parameters

The meaning of "today" is represented in (10), following the architecture of a sign defined in Cooper and Ginzburg (2015). Signs interface with contextual parameters by being dialog game board-aware. For instance, *today* refers to the utterance context parameter *utt-time* and returns the corresponding day. In this way, both the indexical (utterance-time sensitive) and the descriptive (*toDAY*) aspect of "today" are captured.

(10)
$$\left[\begin{array}{ll}
\text{dgb} : & \left[\begin{array}{ll}
\text{spkr} & : \textit{Ind} \\
\text{addr} & : \textit{Ind} \\
\text{utt-time=s-event.s-time} & : \textit{Time} \\
\text{c-utt} & : \text{addressing(spkr,addr,utt-time)}
\end{array}\right] \\
\text{s-event} : & \left[\begin{array}{ll}
\text{phon} & : \text{today} \\
\text{s-time} & : \textit{Time}
\end{array}\right] \\
\text{synsem} : & \left[\begin{array}{ll}
\text{cat = N} : \textit{PoS} & \\
\text{cont} : & \left[\begin{array}{ll}
\text{t} & : \textit{Time} \\
\text{c-day} & : \text{day(t,dgb.utt-time)}
\end{array}\right]
\end{array}\right]
\end{array}\right]$$

In TTR, generalized quantifiers (*Quant*) are of the type of functions from properties (*Ppty*) to record types, where a property is a function from individuals to record types (Cooper, 2013).[7] Hence, "always" cannot apply to "today", since the latter provides an object of basic type *Time* instead of a property.

[6] Using an E-type relational instead of a property abstraction is to be credited to remarks by an anonymous reviewer.

[7] Note that properties defined in this way also cover functions of type $\langle e,e\rangle$ as used above.

However, days underlie a "circle of return": every year has a November 1. Hence, years provide a basis for quantification. It is made available by abstracting away from the indexically given day by means of a function that shifts the context from days to years, call it **calendric coercion**:

(11) $\left[\text{calcoerc} = (\text{r} : \begin{bmatrix}\text{t} & : \textit{Time} \\ \text{c-day} & : \text{day(t,dgb-params.utt-time)}\end{bmatrix}) \begin{bmatrix}\text{y} & : \textit{Time} \\ \text{c-year} & : \text{year(y,r.t)}\end{bmatrix} : (\textit{Rec})\textit{RecType}\right]$

By means of calendric coercion the sentence "Today is always the biggest party day of the year" translates to a general quantifier as in (12) (for details, see Cooper (2013)):

(12) $\begin{bmatrix}\text{q-params} : \begin{bmatrix}\text{restr=calcoerc} : \textit{Ppty} \\ \text{wit} \quad : \text{always}^{\dagger}\text{(restr)}\end{bmatrix} \\ \text{cont} = \begin{bmatrix}\text{scope=big-party-day} \quad : \textit{Ppty} \\ \text{c}_{\text{always}}\text{=}\Uparrow\text{q-params.wit} : \text{always(}\Uparrow\text{dgb-params.restr, scope)}\end{bmatrix} : \textit{Quant}\end{bmatrix}$

The difference between the indexical "today" and a fully resolved calendric expression like "November 1, 2000" is, that the descriptive content of the latter, but not the former, fixes the temporal range from days, over months to years. From this it follows that a partly resolved date expression as in (13) should also allow for calendric coercion, which seems to be correct:

(13) November 1 is always the biggest day of the year.

Turning to another widespread example in this context, namely "I am traditionally allowed to have a last supper". Contrary to the orthodox analysis, it can be argued that actually no descriptive indexical is involved here. This can be seen when the target sentence is contrasted to minimal pair variations:

(14) a. I am traditionally allowed to have a last supper. ⇝ *I, as condemned to death, am traditionally allowed to have a last supper.*

b. I am allowed to have a last supper. ⇝ *I, as condemned to death, am allowed to have a last supper.*

c. Peter is traditionally allowed to have a last supper. ⇝ *Peter, as condemned to death, am traditionally allowed to have a last supper.*

d. Peter is allowed to have a last supper. ⇝ *Peter, as condemned to death, am allowed to have a last supper.*

e. I am allowed to take the bus. ⇝ *I, as buyer of a ticket, are allowed to take the bus.*

f. I am legally allowed to take the bus. ⇝ *I, as buyer of a ticket, are legally allowed to take the bus.*

The systematicity that becomes visible in the examples in (14) suggest that the adverb *traditionally* introduces a social norm according to which the statements are to be judged. In particular, the alleged descriptive readings are independent of indexicals. It is the verb *allow* that introduces a role for the reason of allowance. So, nothing special here, except the need to spell out an appropriate semantics of *traditionally*.

4 Descriptive "I"?

The first person pronoun nonetheless gives rise to *non-speaker referential uses* (King, 2001), as illustrated in Figure 1, due to Kratzer (1978) and Köpping (2017). "I" and "me" in Figure 1 simply pick out the truck and the person carrying the note, respectively. In particular, they do not refer to the speakers, or more generally: the authors, of the tokens, as traditionally assumed ("the referent of 'I' is the speaker of 'I'"). The interpretation of the first person pronoun in the examples is determined by the circumstance of evaluation, not by that of the tokening (Smith, 1989). The referent, however, may still be regarded as the "agent" of the utterance, though the notion of agency is somewhat loose (cf. Kratzer, 1978).

Figure 1: Non-speaker referential uses of the first person pronoun.

A deferred reference interpretation (cf. the respective remarks in Section 2) is possible but fails to account for the straightforward referential type of "I". This is revealed by putting the reprise fragment containing the pronoun to the clarification test (Purver and Ginzburg, 2004). Suppose two people, A and B, are watching the truck passing by. Then one of them might ask for the content of "I" by means of a reprise fragment.

(15) A: *I*? / Who's *I*?
B: The truck, of course.

B's answer in (15) provides evidence for the pronoun referring to the truck without detouring to some metonymic relation. Otherwise B's answer would have to be something like *The guy who wrote the poster* or *The guy who wrote the poster intended it to refer to the truck.*

Such examples can be *described* within a narrow context theory providing a set of indices: the truck instead of token author fills the author slot (Kaplan, 1989; Cohen and Michaelson, 2013). However, comparable to the problem of the link of paycheck interpretations, such an approach does not rule out the token author interpretation, which are not available in such cases.

Remark: the examples involve written inscriptions which are detached from time and place of their production, anyway. Given that written and spoken language are two quite different modes, it may be necessary to distinguish a written and a spoken *I* (likewise for other indexicals). We refrain from follow this line further here, however, noting that things are of course complex: Consider a transporter with a loudspeaker driving through town and the driver advertising via the speakers "I am for rent". Even in this case, the transporter, not the driver, will be taken to the subject of the sentence and thus the referent of the indexical.

The divergence of speaker/author and the meaning of "I" is prominent in literary works. An example is given in (16):

(16) HAMLET: I prithee do not mock me.

The "I" in (16) does not refer to its author (that would be Shakespeare), but to Hamlet, who is indicated to be the "speaker" by means of screenplay typography. Note that the sentence in (16) does not seem to be an instance of quotation: it is Hamlet *speaking*. Compare this to a speaker's act of speaking in a spoken conversation, where the utterance is also not related to its speaker by quotation, but by a causal relation.

Based on these and related considerations, it has been proposed to spell out the semantic rule that fixes the reference of 'I' in terms of the audience, that is, a hearer-oriented construal (Romdenh-Romluc,

2006): "what a speaker can refer to with an indexical utterance is constrained by what an audience can understand" (op. cit., p. 280/1). The loose examples provided here, in particular trying to unify written and spoken data, suggest to spell out an audience-fixing rule in terms of a contiguity relation (holding at the time of perception) between the utterance token (written or spoken) and an entity (the agent). A tentative lexical entry for 'I' is given in (17):

(17)
$$\left[\begin{array}{ll} \text{dgb} : & \left[\begin{array}{ll} \text{ag} & : \mathit{Ind} \\ \text{utt-time=s-event.s-time} & : \mathit{Time} \\ \text{utt-loc} & : \mathit{Loc} \\ \text{c-ctg} & : \text{contiguous(ag,s-event,utt-loc)} \end{array}\right] \\ \text{s-event} : & \left[\begin{array}{ll} \text{phon} & : \text{I} \\ \text{s-time} & : \mathit{Time} \end{array}\right] \\ \text{synsem} : & \left[\begin{array}{ll} \text{cat=Pron} & : \mathit{PoS} \\ \text{cont} & : \left[\text{i=dgb.ag} : \mathit{Ind}\right] \end{array}\right] \end{array}\right]$$

The structure in (17) requires that there is an individual (value of 'ag') which stands in a contiguity relation to the utterance token of "I" (indicated by the 's-event' being an argument of the contiguity relation 'c-ctg'). The semantic contribution 'cont' of the first person pronoun is referential: it is the individual found at label 'ag'. As a matter of fact, the contiguity relation in most cases just picks out the "classical speaker" ("ag=spkr"). After all, lip movements and their role in the causal relationship to perceptible speech sounds in spoken conversation provide good evidence for the respective contiguity relation (cf. e.g. Kubovy and Schutz, 2010).

5 Conclusion

It has been argued that the challenge of fixing the reference of descriptive "today" can be solved by means of an operation called calendric coercion. The re-interpretation of indexicals is triggered by type mismatches induced in quantificational contexts. Thus, the model sketched here only makes use of familiar coercion operations and exploits a grammar-utterance situation interface of situated communication.

Furthermore, following audience-oriented semantic accounts to the first person pronoun from philosophy of language, a contiguity rule for "I" has been proposed, which allows for a semantic description of cases that often have been explained in terms of a metonymic process. However, there seem to at least two problems with a philosophical account like the one sketched above. Searching for a generalized semantic rule that covers all uses, in particular the descriptive ones, reduces the reference fixing content of indexicals to very broad notions (like "contiguity", as suggested above). These notion in turn require explanations themselves. Secondly, even the contiguity rule falls short in cases where a truck carries a note like "Marry me!", which obviously does not refer to the truck. Resorting to different ways of context-dependence of indexicals seems to be more adequate.

References

Cohen, J. and E. Michaelson (2013). Indexicality and the answering machine paradox. *Philosophy Compass 8*(6), 580–592.

Cooper, R. (2012). Type theory and semantics in flux. In R. Kempson, T. Fernando, and N. Asher (Eds.), *Philosophy of Linguistics*, Volume 14 of *Handbook of Philosophy of Science*, pp. 271–323. Oxford and Amsterdam: Elsevier.

Cooper, R. (2013). Clarification and generalized quantifiers. *Dialogue & Discourse 4*(1), 1–25.

Cooper, R. and J. Ginzburg (2015). Type theory with records for natural language semantics. In S. Lappin and C. Fox (Eds.), *The Handbook of Contemporary Semantic Theory* (2 ed.)., Chapter 12, pp. 375–407. Oxford, UK: Wiley-Blackwell.

Dowty, D. R. (1981). Quantification and the lexicon: a reply to Fodor and Fodor. In M. Moortgat, H. van der Hulst, and T. Hoekstra (Eds.), *The Scope of Lexical Rules*, Linguistic Models, pp. 79–106. Dordrecht and Cinnaminson: FORIS Publications.

Elbourne, P. (2001). E-type anaphora as NP-deletion. *Natural Language Semantics 9*(3), 241–288.

Elbourne, P. (2008). Demonstratives as individual concepts. *Linguistics and Philosophy 31*(4), 409–466.

Ginzburg, J. (2012). *The Interactive Stance: Meaning for Conversation.* Oxford, UK: Oxford University Press.

Heim, I. (1990). E-type pronouns and donkey anaphora. *Linguistics and Philosophy 13*, 137–177.

Kaplan, D. (1989). Demonstratives. In J. Almog, J. Perry, and H. Wettstein (Eds.), *Themes from Kaplan*, pp. 481–563. New York and Oxford: Oxford University Press.

Keenan, E. (2011). Quantifiers. In C. Maienborn, K. von Heusinger, and P. Portner (Eds.), *Semantics: an International Handbook of Natural Language Meaning*, Volume 2 of *Handbücher zur Sprach- und Kommunikationswissenschaft*, Chapter 43, pp. 1058–1087. De Gruyter Mouton.

Kijania-Placek, K. (2015). Descriptive indexicals, propositional attitudes and the double role of context. In *Modeling and Using Context: Proceedings of the 9th International and Interdisciplinary Conference*, CONTEXT 2015, pp. 287–301.

King, J. C. (2001). *Complex Demonstratives: A Quantificational Account*, Volume 2 of *Contemporary Philosophical Monographs.* Cambridge, MA: MIT Press.

Köpping, J. (2017). On individuating contexts (and indices). Logisch-semantisches Kolloquium, Thomas Ede Zimmermann, Goethe-Universität Frankfurt.

Kratzer, A. (1978). *Semantik der Rede: Kontexttheorie, Modalwörter, Konditionalsätze.* Monographien: Linguistik und Kommunikationswissenschaft. Königstein/Ts.: Scriptor.

Kubovy, M. and M. Schutz (2010). Audio-visual objects. *Review of Philosophy and Psychology 1*(1), 41–61.

Nunberg, G. (1993). Indexicality and deixis. *Linguistics and Philosophy 16*(1), 1–43.

Nunberg, G. (2004). Descriptive indexicals and indexical descriptions. In M. Reimer and A. Bezuidenhout (Eds.), *Descriptions and Beyond*, Chapter 6, pp. 261–279. Oxford: Clarendon Press.

Pedersen, W. (2011). Implicit arguments, paychecks and variable-free semantics. *Semantics and Linguistic Theory 21*, 155–175.

Purver, M. and J. Ginzburg (2004). Clarifying noun phrase semantics. *Journal of Semantics 21*(3), 283–339.

Romdenh-Romluc, K. (2006). 'I'. *Philosophical Studies 128*(2), 257–283.

Smith, Q. (1989). The multiple uses of indexicals. *Synthese 78*(2), 167–191.

Umbach, C. and H. Gust (2014). Similarity demonstratives. *Lingua 149*, 74–93. SI: Modification at the Interfaces.

Creating Common Ground through Multimodal Simulations

James Pustejovsky[1], Nikhil Krishnaswamy[1], Bruce Draper[2], Pradyumna Narayana[2], and Rahul Bangar[2]

[1]Department of Computer Science, Brandeis University, Waltham, MA, USA
[2]Department of Computer Science, Colorado State University, Fort Collins, CO, USA
{jamesp,nkrishna}@brandeis.edu
{draper,prady,rahul.bangar}@colostate.edu

Abstract

The demand for more sophisticated human-computer interactions is rapidly increasing, as users become more accustomed to conversation-like interactions with their devices. In this paper, we examine this changing landscape in the context of human-machine interaction in a shared workspace to achieve a common goal. In our prototype system, people and avatars cooperate to build blocks world structures through the interaction of language, gesture, vision, and action. This provides a platform to study computational issues involved in multimodal communication. In order to establish elements of the common ground in discourse between speakers, we have created an embodied 3D simulation, enabling both the generation and interpretation of multiple modalities, including: language, gesture, and the visualization of objects moving and agents acting in their environment. The simulation is built on the modeling language VoxML, that encodes objects with rich semantic typing and action affordances, and actions themselves as multimodal programs, enabling contextually salient inferences and decisions in the environment. We illustrate this with a walk-through of multimodal communication in a shared task.

1 Introduction

In this paper, we discuss a developing approach towards modeling peer-to-peer communication using multiple modalities, e.g., language, gesture, vision, and action. This platform integrates a multimodal model of semantics (*Multimodal Semantic Simulations, MSS)* (Pustejovsky and Krishnaswamy, 2016; Krishnaswamy et al., 2017) with a realtime vision system for recognizing human gestures (Wang et al., 2017). This framework assumes both a richer formal model of events and their participants, as well as a modeling language for constructing 3D visualizations of objects and events denoted by linguistic expressions. We position this approach in the context of the questions posed by the workshop organizers, and provide more detail into the architecture that integrates the multiple sources of knowledge within the shared context of communication.

To begin with, let us distinguish between experience and action: two individuals who share an experience, such as witnessing a natural event, hearing a clap of thunder, or feeling the earth tremor, are jointly "co-perceiving an event". Hence, they are *co-situated* and *co-perceptive*. If these two beings are communicating in order to carry out a shared task, such as building a structure, moving objects, or clearing a space, then they can be considered "agents", who are not only co-perceiving the present situation and subsequent situations as they change, but are also acting, together or individually, as a result of communicative interactions. Hence, what is being shared in the latter is considerably richer and more complex in character. Namely, there is agreement, acceptance, or recognition of a common goal between the agents, what can be called "co-intent". These combined factors constitute the first aspects of is called "common ground": namely, co-situatedness, co-perception, and co-intent. The theory of common ground has a rich and diverse literature concerning what is shared or presupposed in human communication (Clark et al., 1991; Gilbert, 1992; Stalnaker, 2002; Asher, 1998; Tomasello and Carpenter, 2007).

When engaged in accomplishing a task jointly, agents share one additional anchoring strategy that greatly enhances the expressiveness of common ground: namely, the ability to "co-attend". Because of the inherently directed nature of attention and co-attention, we will, rather, speak of a "shared situated reference" in the discussion that follows. This ability will emerge as central to determining the denotations of participants in shared events. Events as we experience them are distinct from the way we refer to them with language. The mechanisms in language allow us to package, quantify, measure, and order our experiences, creating rich conceptual reifications and semantic differentiations. The surface realization of this ability is mostly manifest through our linguistic utterances, but is also witnessed through gestures. By examining the nature of the common ground assumed in communication, we can study the conceptual expressiveness of these systems (Pustejovsky, 2018).

We believe that simulation can play a crucial role in human-computer communication; it creates a shared epistemic model of the environment inhabited by a human and an artificial agent, and demonstrates the knowledge held by the agent publicly. Demonstrating knowledge is needed to ensure a shared understanding with the humans involved in the activity, but why create a simulation model, if the goal is to interact with an avatar or robot? If a robotic agent is able to receive linguistic information from a human commander or collaborator and interpret that relative to its current physical circumstances, it can create an epistemic representation of that same information. However, without a modality to express that representation independently, the human is unable to verify or query what the robotic agent is perceiving or how that perception is being interpreted. In a simulation environment the human and robot share an epistemic space, and any modality of communication that can be expressed within that space (e.g., linguistic, visual, gestural) enriches the number of ways that a human and a robotic agent can communicate within object and situation-based tasks, such as those investigated by Hsiao et al. (2008), Dzifcak et al. (2009), Cangelosi (2010).

The simulation environment provided by our model includes the perceptual domain of objects, properties, and events. In addition, propositional content in the model is accessible to the discourse, allowing access to beliefs, desires, and intentions (BDI), and for them to be distinguished by the agents to act and communicate appropriately. This provides the non-linguistic visual and action modalities, which are augmented by the inherently non-linguistic gestural modality enacted within the visual context.

As gesture is intended for visual interpretation, it is directly interpretable in the co-visual context if and only if the denotation of its interpretation function is directly available in the simulation through visual inspection (Lascarides and Stone (2006, 2009); Clair et al. (2010); Matuszek et al. (2014)). Direction or vector information encoded in a gesture hooks into direct deixis and satisfiable actions by projecting the gesture onto a distinct area of the simulation environment. For entity descriptions, speech allows for a randomly accessible and indexable descriptions, while gesture allows for physically and spatially grounded regions, objects, or configurations. Speech can express nominal, qualitative, tangible, or non-tangible attributes, while gesture is limited to orientation and direction, shape, size, relative distance, and manner of motion. For communicative events, where speech allows for any mood (declarative, interrogative, imperative), gesture is usually imperative, except for speech acts. Speech allows for an essentially unconstrained expression of propositional content, while gesture is limited to the propositional content of a speech act, and the content of a deixis or action description.

For explicit spatial grounding, gesture is computationally advantageous as spatially-encoded information in the gesture (e.g., direction, vector, etc.) can be directly grounded in the scene without having to process an additional linguistic layer of indirection. In some cases, spatially-denoting manner is easier to model with gesture than language. This is also the case with technology-driven multimodal display interfaces (Johnston, 2009), but here we are concerned with a co-situated situation where the interlocutors, human and virtual, share an epistemic space.

We assume interlocutors have explicit and distinct modes of interpretation as accessed through perception. Input from the environment (our embedding space) evidences various beliefs that we establish as knowledge. Our model of synthetic vision provides distinct but mutually coherent views on the shared environment. An example involving object occlusion is discussed in Section 3.

Any of the different modalities in our model can be used to disambiguate new information introduced into the context by the other participant(s) by enumerating possible options, pruning question/answer steps based on the number of options, and interaction between interlocutors until an unambiguous interpretation is achieved. Examples of this are discussed in Section 4.

2 Multimodal Communication

2.1 Language

Our system uses VoxSim, an open-source language-driven event simulator (Krishnaswamy and Pustejovsky, 2016a,b) to operationalize events in real time, mapping from natural language input using a dynamic semantics and the modeling language VoxML (Pustejovsky and Krishnaswamy, 2016). VoxML semantic typing extends that provided within Generative Lexicon Theory (Pustejovsky, 1995), as well as the approach taken in Asher (2011), to enable a semantics of embodiment (Pustejovsky, 2013; Pustejovsky and Krishnaswamy, 2014). Embodiment, a requirement on and facilitated by the shared virtual environment, allows us to operationalize gestures as programs enacted within the 3D environment with a direct mapping to linguistic description. This enactment is performed by a virtual avatar, in the vein of prior work studying human-computer communication (Kopp et al., 2003; Sowa and Kopp, 2003; Kopp et al., 2005; Krämer et al., 2007; Weitnauer et al., 2008).

2.2 Gesture

Gestures and actions are the primary modes of communication between a person and an avatar in our system. The human user stands at one end of a table, facing a monitor at the other end showing a virtual continuation of the table, and the avatar. The user's motions are captured using a Microsoft Kinect v2 RGBD sensor. Gestures are detected in real time using in-house gesture recognition software (in press) and sent to the avatar via VoxSim. The avatar's gestures are displayed to the human on the monitor.

The real-time gesture detection system can recognize 34 hand poses trained from a publicly available dataset of naturally occurring gestures between human subjects working on blocks world tasks (Wang et al., 2017). It can also detect head nods, head shakes, stepping up to or back from the table, as well as the directions of arm motions. Other body poses not classified by the recognizer as one or the above are labeled "other," and not considered to be semantic gestures in this context.

Our prototype scenarios restrict the gestural lexicon to only eight gestural voxemes (visual lexemes), four of which pertain to actions and four to the state of discourse. The action-based gestural voxemes are: *point* (i.e., deixis), either at a block or open space; *grab*, the user mimicking grabbing a block; *carry*, mimicking moving a block they have grabbed; and *push*. *Point, carry* and *push* include directionality (e.g., "left" or "away"). The dialogue-based voxemes are: *engage* and *disengage*, to begin and end a dialogue; and *positive* and *negative acknowledge*, to signal agreement or disagreement.

Gestural voxemes, as we use the term here, are more general than physical gestures. For example, users can signal positive acknowledgement by nodding their heads or by giving a "thumbs up" sign with either or both hands. There are therefore seven different motions to signify positive acknowledgement (including combinations of nodding and thumbs up with either or both hands). Each voxeme therefore corresponds to a set of synonym gestures, often including but not limited to **enantiomorphs**. As the semantics of gesture are often culturally and situationally conditioned (Müller, 2004), we should note that the gesture set used here comes from a dataset elicited from United States university students (i.e., WEIRD (Henrich et al., 2010)), and used in a context designed to achieve a particular construction goal, and that should be taken into account and considering their descriptive properties, creation, and enactment (Streeck, 2008, 2009).

2.3 Synthetic Vision

In the context of peer-to-peer communication, we are concerned not only with co-belief associated with presupposed and shared communal knowledge (Grosz and Sidner, 1990; Cohen et al., 1990; Asher and Lascarides, 2008; Lascarides and Asher, 2009), but also that knowledge arising through the shared experiences of co-situated (but distinct) perceptions. For this (and other) reasons, perception reports have often been modeled modally as a conventional epistemic operator (Shoham and Del Val, 1991), yet while this is a formal convenience it is not cognitively or computationally realistic (Musto and Konolige, 1993; Bell and Huang, 1998). This has been a gap in approaches to perception through modal logic, reducing the act of perception to a extramission theory of vision. Alternatively, while computational approaches to vision explicitly operationalize the recognition of features and objects, this is far from our goal of extracting epistemic relations from a scene. Some formal approaches have moved beyond these views, by acknowledging the role of sensory capture as distinct from the propositional content that results from this act (Wooldridge and Lomuscio, 1999), as well as (Schwarzentruber, 2010, 2011). We share this view, but aim to go further, by embedding the modal interpretation of the knowledge associated with perception as the result of a signal transmission from sensory data in the environment.

To this end, we adopt the strategies and modeling techniques of synthetic vision (Noser et al., 1995; Peters and O'Sullivan, 2002) combined with work in dynamic epistemic logic (Goranko and Otto, 2007; Plaza, 2007; Van Benthem, 2011). We distinguish between egocentric (viewer-based) and allocentric (externally-based) perspectives. Within a 3D environment, the problem of visibility is introduced because objects may be occluded from the frame of reference of the viewer. Further, because of distinct egocentric frames of reference (FoR) for each interlocutor in a co-situated, co-perceptual task, we need to track the interpretations (valuations) of qualitative spatial relations that rely on FoR, such as *in front of*, *to the left*, *behind*, etc. (Zimmermann and Freksa, 1996; Ligozat, 1993).

We implement an evidential-based model of perception, where knowledge is arrived at or "evidenced through" inferences over properties and relations from sensory input, with which we define $\mathcal{S}_a\phi$ (agent a sees that ϕ). Synthetic vision, $\mathcal{S}_a\phi$, for a computational agent within VoxSim is defined, in part, as a relation of *Evidences* ($\mathcal{E}$), given informally as follows: $\psi\mathcal{E}_a\phi$ states that a sensory input relation, ψ, provides enough evidence for agent a to know that ϕ. The set of evidencing propositions includes the following object attribute classes: *color*, *shape*, *size*, and *orientation*. For two or more objects, the qualitative spatial relations from RCC8 and RCC-3D (Randell et al., 1992; Albath et al., 2010) are used, along with orientational (directional) relations.

2.4 Action

At any point in the human-avatar interaction where the avatar's internal logic has extracted a meaning from the linguistic or gestural input, the avatar then communicates this understanding to the human by performing the associated action, such as pushing a block adjacent to another block, putting a block on top of another block, or moving a block into a specified region of the table.

Action can demonstrate clear, unambiguous understanding, such as moving a distinct block to a definite location, or can be a request for more meaning, as when the avatar can gesture toward a block it thinks *might* have been indicated by the human, in order to request confirmation.

Action therefore communicates the avatar's understanding of the current situational context, providing an epistemic basis that each party can perform inference over to bring their understanding of the other's vision of the external world into line.

3 Example Scenario and Walk-through

Figure 1 illustrates the same configuration of blocks as seen from the perspectives of the human and avatar. From the avatar's point of view (POV), the green block is occluded by the larger red block.

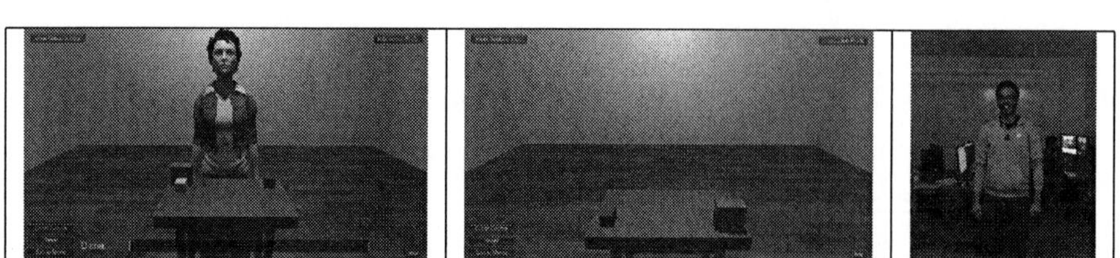

Figure 1: L: Human's view of scene; C: Avatar's view of blocks, table; R: Avatar's view of human

Using this configuration, an example scenario follows as depicted in Figure 2, with individual interactions indicated by the labeled frames which show the human's action in the left half of the frame and the avatar's action on the right.

When the human begins by pointing to his left (Frame A), this is interpreted unambiguously as indicating the red block, as the avatar cannot see the green one.

The human moves his left hand, palm open, from his left to his right, indicating "push to right" (Frame B). Here, the avatar enters a disambiguation loop, a state machine of which is shown in Figure 3. Using both text and audio output in natural language, the avatar requests a clarification: Does the human intend her to push the indicated (red) block adjacent to the (blue) block on the right side of the table? This is confirmed by a thumbs-up gesture from the human, and the avatar moves the red block to the left side of the blue block (Frame C).

This action has an effect unintended by the avatar: moving the red block has exposed the green one, the existence of which was previously unknown to the avatar. Before this point, the human and avatar are co-situated in and co-perceptive of the scene, but their respective visions of the external world do not cohere due to their differing beliefs regarding the existence of the green block. Now, when the green block is revealed to the avatar, they have the same beliefs about the three blocks in the scene, and the avatar must update her internal model of the scene to include the existence of the green block. The prior existence of the green block to this point is also included in the update axiomatically. Having global knowledge of the scene, we can see that the two agents' models of the world are now coherent, through an update facilitated by multimodal interaction.

Now that knowledge of the existence and location of the green block is common to both parties, when the human indicates (his) left side of the table, the avatar can unambiguously understand this to mean that the green block is indicated (Frame D). By then gesturing *grab* (hand in a clawlike position, as shown in Frame E), then moving his hand up, over to the red block, and down, the human can indicate to the avatar that he wants her to pick up the green block and move it either on top of the red block, or into the same region of the table, an ambiguity that the avatar can resolve though some questions, answered and acknowledged by the human. The result is a four-step staircase made of three blocks (Frame F).

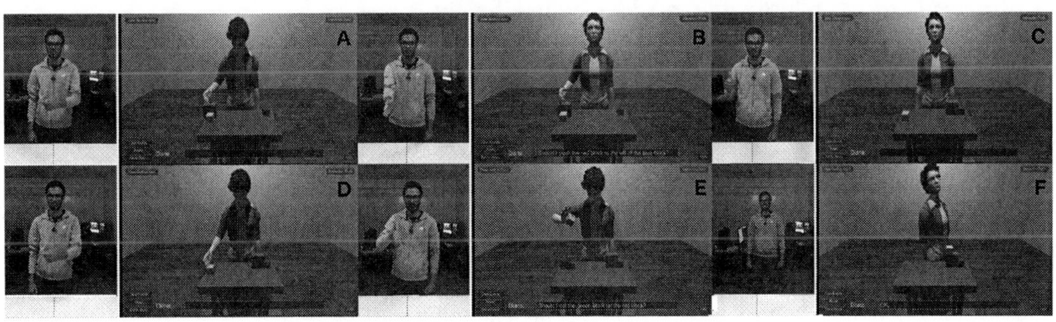

Figure 2: Example staircase construction scenario

Our model of communication allows for multiple parameters to be altered in order to make changes to the nature of the interaction. For example, the avatar can behave more proactively or less when disambiguating gestures, which can affect the action taken. Examples of this are discussed in Section 4.

4 Implications for Human-Computer Communication

Co-situatedness and co-perception of the participants give rise to some interesting considerations in their interaction. When, in the example from Section 3, the avatar begins moving the red block and reveals the green block, she might pause her move before completion and clarify that moving the red block was actually what the human intended; the introduction of the green block into her present model of the world causes her to update her past model, as discussed in Section 3, and the propagation of that dynamic epistemic model to the present creates a choice-point where none existed before.

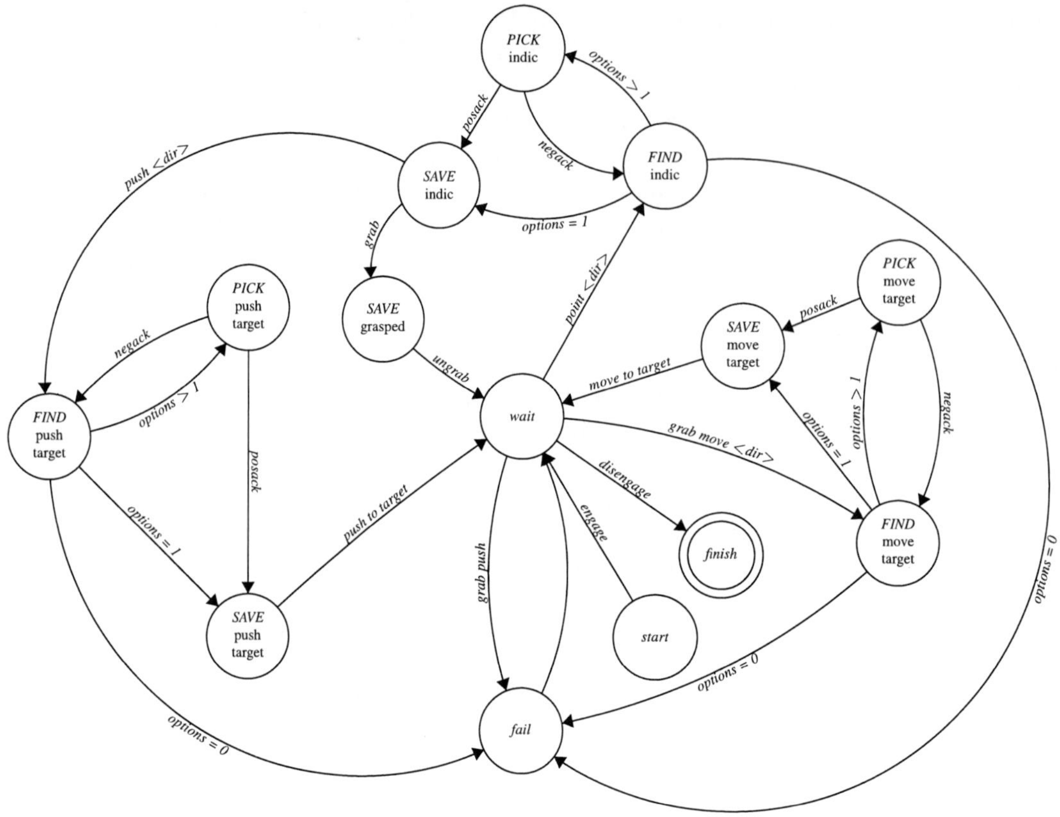

Figure 3: Finite state machine for dialogue management

Alternately, when the avatar reaches for or starts moving the red block before the green block is revealed, the human might interrupt with a "stop" gesture or utterance, indicating that the avatar is doing something divergent from the human's plans. Evidenced by the positions of the blocks and the actions being taken with them, the avatar can infer that the indicated block is not the one she is supposed to be affecting; since no other blocks are visible in the originally-indicated region of the table, this introduces the possibility that there exists another block to be manipulated. The avatar's model of the scenario changes from a two-block model $\models r, b$ at t_0 to a three-block model $\models r, g, b$ at t_n, where new information is introduced either by evidencing or inference in a logic of synthetic vision. This way we can represent psychological phenomena like object permanence in a simulation environment as changes in the entropy of the information available to the virtual agent through its (synthetic) vision of the scene.

5 Conclusion

Multimodal peer-to-peer interfaces require robust integration of conversational modalities in a naturalistic fashion. Here we outline the first steps toward such integration, based on the logic of a multimodal simulation semantics and 3D environment as the platform for shared common ground. We provide our computational agent with a framework for some of the faculties natively available to humans using sophisticated computer vision techniques to recognize gesture and by laying the groundwork for a modal logic of synthetic vision. The result is a framework and platform that interweaves linguistic and non-linguistic modalities to facilitate the completion of a shared task by exploiting the relative strengths of linguistic and non-linguistic context to exchange information in a situated communication.

Acknowledgements

We would like to thank the reviewers for their insightful comments. We have tried to incorporate their suggestions where possible. This work was supported by Contract W911NF-15-C-0238 with the US Defense Advanced Research Projects Agency (DARPA) and the Army Research Office (ARO). Approved for Public Release, Distribution Unlimited. The views expressed herein are ours and do not reflect the official policy or position of the Department of Defense or the U.S. Government. All errors and mistakes are, of course, the responsibilities of the authors.

References

Albath, J., J. L. Leopold, C. L. Sabharwal, and A. M. Maglia (2010). RCC-3D: Qualitative spatial reasoning in 3D. In *CAINE*, pp. 74–79.

Asher, N. (1998). Common ground, corrections and coordination. *Journal of Semantics*.

Asher, N. (2011). *Lexical meaning in context: A web of words*. Cambridge University Press.

Asher, N. and A. Lascarides (2008). Commitments, beliefs and intentions in dialogue. *Proceedings of Londial*, 35–42.

Bell, J. and Z. Huang (1998). Seeing is believing. In *4th Symposium on Logical Formalizations of Commonsense Reasoning (Commonsense 98)*.

Cangelosi, A. (2010). Grounding language in action and perception: from cognitive agents to humanoid robots. *Physics of life reviews* 7(2), 139–151.

Clair, A. S., R. Mead, M. J. Matarić, et al. (2010). Monitoring and guiding user attention and intention in human-robot interaction. In *ICRA-ICAIR Workshop, Anchorage, AK, USA*, Volume 1025.

Clark, H. H., S. E. Brennan, et al. (1991). Grounding in communication. *Perspectives on socially shared cognition 13*(1991), 127–149.

Cohen, P. R., J. L. Morgan, and M. E. Pollack (1990). *Intentions in communication*. MIT press.

Dzifcak, J., M. Scheutz, C. Baral, and P. Schermerhorn (2009). What to do and how to do it: Translating natural language directives into temporal and dynamic logic representation for goal management and action execution. In *Robotics and Automation, 2009. ICRA'09. IEEE International Conference on*, pp. 4163–4168. IEEE.

Gilbert, M. (1992). *On social facts*. Princeton University Press.

Goranko, V. and M. Otto (2007). 5 model theory of modal logic. *Studies in Logic and Practical Reasoning 3*, 249–329.

Grosz, B. J. and C. L. Sidner (1990). Plans for discourse. In *Intentions in communication*. MIT Press.

Henrich, J., S. J. Heine, and A. Norenzayan (2010). Most people are not weird. *Nature 466*(7302), 29–29.

Hsiao, K.-Y., S. Tellex, S. Vosoughi, R. Kubat, and D. Roy (2008). Object schemas for grounding language in a responsive robot. *Connection Science 20*(4), 253–276.

Johnston, M. (2009). Building multimodal applications with emma. In *Proceedings of the 2009 international conference on Multimodal interfaces*, pp. 47–54. ACM.

Kopp, S., L. Gesellensetter, N. C. Krämer, and I. Wachsmuth (2005). A conversational agent as museum guide–design and evaluation of a real-world application. In *International Workshop on Intelligent Virtual Agents*, pp. 329–343. Springer.

Kopp, S., T. Sowa, and I. Wachsmuth (2003). Imitation games with an artificial agent: From mimicking to understanding shape-related iconic gestures. In *International Gesture Workshop*, pp. 436–447. Springer.

Krämer, N. C., N. Simons, and S. Kopp (2007). The effects of an embodied conversational agents nonverbal behavior on users evaluation and behavioral mimicry. In *International Workshop on Intelligent Virtual Agents*, pp. 238–251. Springer.

Krishnaswamy, N., P. Narayana, I. Wang, K. Rim, R. Bangar, D. Patil, G. Mulay, J. Ruiz, R. Beveridge, B. Draper, and J. Pustejovsky (2017). Communicating and acting: Understanding gesture in simulation semantics. In *12th International Workshop on Computational Semantics*.

Krishnaswamy, N. and J. Pustejovsky (2016a). Multimodal semantic simulations of linguistically underspecified motion events. In *Spatial Cognition X: International Conference on Spatial Cognition*. Springer.

Krishnaswamy, N. and J. Pustejovsky (2016b). VoxSim: A visual platform for modeling motion language. In *Proceedings of COLING 2016, the 26th International Conference on Computational Linguistics: Technical Papers*. ACL.

Lascarides, A. and N. Asher (2009). Agreement, disputes and commitments in dialogue. *Journal of Semantics 26*(2), 109–158.

Lascarides, A. and M. Stone (2006). Formal semantics for iconic gesture. In *Proceedings of the 10th Workshop on the Semantics and Pragmatics of Dialogue (BRANDIAL)*, pp. 64–71.

Lascarides, A. and M. Stone (2009). A formal semantic analysis of gesture. *Journal of Semantics 26*(4), 393–449.

Ligozat, G. (1993). Qualitative triangulation for spatial reasoning. *Spatial Information Theory A Theoretical Basis for GIS*, 54–68.

Matuszek, C., L. Bo, L. Zettlemoyer, and D. Fox (2014). Learning from unscripted deictic gesture and language for human-robot interactions. In *AAAI*, pp. 2556–2563.

Müller, C. (2004). Forms and uses of the palm up open hand: A case of a gesture family. *The semantics and pragmatics of everyday gestures 9*, 233–256.

Musto, D. and K. Konolige (1993). Reasoning about perception. *AI Communications 6*(3-4), 207–212.

Noser, H., O. Renault, D. Thalmann, and N. M. Thalmann (1995). Navigation for digital actors based on synthetic vision, memory, and learning. *Computers & graphics 19*(1), 7–19.

Peters, C. and C. O'Sullivan (2002). Synthetic vision and memory for autonomous virtual humans. In *Computer Graphics Forum*, Volume 21, pp. 743–752. Wiley Online Library.

Plaza, J. (2007). Logics of public communications. *Synthese 158*(2), 165.

Pustejovsky, J. (1995). *The Generative Lexicon*. MIT Press, Cambridge, MA.

Pustejovsky, J. (2013). Dynamic event structure and habitat theory. In *Proceedings of the 6th International Conference on Generative Approaches to the Lexicon (GL2013)*, pp. 1–10. ACL.

Pustejovsky, J. (2018). From experiencing events in the action-perception cycle to representing events in language. *Interaction Studies 19.*

Pustejovsky, J. and N. Krishnaswamy (2014). Generating simulations of motion events from verbal descriptions. *Lexical and Computational Semantics (* SEM 2014)*, 99.

Pustejovsky, J. and N. Krishnaswamy (2016, May). VoxML: A visualization modeling language. In N. C. C. Chair), K. Choukri, T. Declerck, S. Goggi, M. Grobelnik, B. Maegaard, J. Mariani, H. Mazo, A. Moreno, J. Odijk, and S. Piperidis (Eds.), *Proceedings of the Tenth International Conference on Language Resources and Evaluation (LREC 2016)*, Paris, France. European Language Resources Association (ELRA).

Randell, D., Z. Cui, and A. Cohn (1992). A spatial logic based on regions and connections. In M. Kaufmann (Ed.), *Proceedings of the 3rd International Conference on Knowledge Representation and Reasoning*, San Mateo, pp. 165–176.

Schwarzentruber, F. (2010). *Seeing, knowing, doing: case studies in modal logic.* Ph. D. thesis, Université de Toulouse, Université Toulouse III-Paul Sabatier.

Schwarzentruber, F. (2011). Seeing, knowledge and common knowledge. In *LORI*, pp. 258–271.

Shoham, Y. and A. Del Val (1991). *A logic for perception and belief.* Department of Computer Science, Stanford University.

Sowa, T. and S. Kopp (2003). A cognitive model for the representation and processing of shape-related gestures. In *Proceedings of the European Cognitive Science Conference (EuroCogSci03)*, pp. 441.

Stalnaker, R. (2002). Common ground. *Linguistics and philosophy 25*(5), 701–721.

Streeck, J. (2008). Depicting by gesture. *Gesture 8*(3), 285–301.

Streeck, J. (2009). *Gesturecraft: The manu-facture of meaning*, Volume 2. John Benjamins Publishing.

Tomasello, M. and M. Carpenter (2007). Shared intentionality. *Developmental science 10*(1), 121–125.

Van Benthem, J. (2011). *Logical dynamics of information and interaction.* Cambridge University Press.

Wang, I., M. Ben Fraj, P. Narayana, D. Patil, G. Mulay, R. Bangar, R. Beveridge, B. Draper, and J. Ruiz (2017). Eggnog: A continuous, multi-modal data set of naturally occurring gestures with ground truth labels. In *Proceedings of the 12th IEEE International Conference on Automatic Face & Gesture Recognition.*

Wang, I., P. Narayana, D. Patil, G. Mulay, R. Bangar, B. Draper, R. Beveridge, and J. Ruiz (2017). Exploring the use of gesture in collaborative tasks. In *Proceedings of the 2017 CHI Conference Extended Abstracts on Human Factors in Computing Systems*, CHI EA '17, New York, NY, USA, pp. 2990–2997. ACM.

Weitnauer, E., N. M. Thomas, F. Rabe, and S. Kopp (2008). Intelligent agents living in social virtual environments–bringing max into second life. In *International Workshop on Intelligent Virtual Agents*, pp. 552–553. Springer.

Wooldridge, M. and A. Lomuscio (1999). Reasoning about visibility, perception, and knowledge. In *International Workshop on Agent Theories, Architectures, and Languages*, pp. 1–12. Springer.

Zimmermann, K. and C. Freksa (1996). Qualitative spatial reasoning using orientation, distance, and path knowledge. *Applied intelligence 6*(1), 49–58.

Text-Picture Relations in Multimodal Instructions

Ielka van der Sluis Anne Nienke Eppinga
Gisela Redeker
Center for Language and Cognition Groningen
University of Groningen
{i.f.van.der.sluis}{g.redeker}@rug.nl

Abstract

This paper presents a multi-method approach to the description and evaluation of multimodal content in situated contexts. First, a corpus of 15 simple first-aid instructions that include texts and pictures is shown to exhibit variation in content and presentation. We then report a user study in which four versions of a tick-removal instruction were used to test the effects of the relative placement of text and pictures in a particular instruction. The participants' processing of the instruction and their task performance were video-recorded and registered with an eye tracker. Questionnaires and interviews were used to measure comprehension, recall and the instruction's attractiveness. Results show that users first read at least some of the text before looking at the pictures, and prefer to have the pictures placed to the right or below the text.

1 Introduction and Background

In document design research the combination of text and pictures has been noted but not so much investigated in terms of function and content (cf. Schriver, 1997). Although useful starting points have been provided (Bateman, 2014; Aouladomar, 2005), we are unaware of a standard methodology to describe and evaluate text-picture relations in situated use. This leaves document designers without specific guidelines, while users may experience difficulties in effectively processing multimodal content due to mismatches with their expectations and cognitive capacities. Various models (Schnotz et al., 2017; Sweller, 2016; Mayer, 2005; Schnotz, 2005) and empirical studies (van Hooijdonk and Krahmer, 2008; Houts et al., 2006; Katz et al., 2006; Maes et al., 2004) suggest that functional pictorial content benefits processing content in general. In this paper we explore a method in which we first describe and subsequently evaluate multimodal content to specify the exact text-picture relations that serve this enhanced processing. The research question that we aim to answer is: How can we identify the relations between text and pictures that influence the quality of multimodal content presentations?

In this paper we concentrate on multimodal first-aid instructions. Multimodal instructions (MIs) include pictures and text and instruct users to perform procedural tasks. Consequently, MIs allow evaluation of comprehension and recall not only through reading and judging, but also via assessment of situated use (cf. the discussion in Van der Sluis, Leito & Redeker, 2016). We present a corpus analysis (Section 2) to explore the variation between existing MI designs and to determine which text-picture relations may affect the MI quality. We present a user study (Section 3) in which multiple methods are employed to evaluate particular document designs and to inform annotation models for multimodal content. We conclude and discuss the outcomes and future directions (Section 4).

2 Corpus Study

A small corpus of 15 Dutch tick-removal instructions was collected from public online sources. The instructions were selected to contain both text and pictures, i.e. they were multimodal instructions (MIs). For comparability, the selected MIs described and depicted the procedure with tweezers, not with dedicated tick-removal tools. Figures 1 and 2 present two examples to illustrate the variation in the corpus (e.g., position of text and pictures, number of steps, amount of text per step, inclusion of additional information in either text or pictures). The corpus annotation was developed and refined in close discussion between the authors of this paper, with the second author taking the lead in the majority of the analyses in the context of her MA thesis (Eppinga, 2017).

Figure 1: MI14 - www.ggddrenthe.nl

Figure 2: MI15 - www.serviceapotheek.nl

2.1 Description of Text

The MI texts were analysed in terms of composition (e.g., textual elements, layout), general characteristics (e.g., title, number of steps, number of sentences), actions (status: preparatory, core or closing; aspect: process or result) and control information (e.g., warning, conditional, motivation, explanation, extra information).

Composition: Three genre-specific textual elements were distinguished: preamble, actual instruction, and closing. Figure 2, for instance, includes a preamble (ie., the first two sentences), the actual instruction (here, five steps) and a closing (ie., two sentences that advise the user to visit a docter if the victim feels ill in the three months after the tick was removed). Only three of the 15 MIs in our corpus did not start with a preamble; in all others, all three textual elements were identified. Text-structuring layout elements such as white space and horizontal lines, and paragraph numbering were noted.

General Text Characteristics: All fifteen MIs in our corpus include a title. These titles usually concern the removal of a tick (e.g., MI1: 'Wat te doen bij een tekenbeet', what to do in the case of a tick; MI11 'Hoe een teek verwijderen', How to remove a tick). Sometimes however the title addresses a particular audience, for instance, in the case of MI13 'Instructie over risico's bij werken in het groen' (Instruction about risks for gardeners). MI13 also includes a subtitle that is more specific ('Ziekte van Lyme: een teek verwijderen', Lyme disease: removing a tick). No other instances of subtitles were discovered. Sometimes the title is quite generic (e.g., M17: Wat kunt u zelf doen om overlast te voorkomen?', What can you do to avoid any inconvenience?). The number of steps in the MIs varies from two to ten ($M = 5.5$, $std = 1.68$). The number of sentences varies from seven to ten ($M = 11.4$, $std = 3.22$). The number of words varies from 110 to 275 ($M = 163.01$, $std = 43.29$).

Actions: The actions included in the actual instruction were classified as preparatory actions (e.g., pick up tweezers), core actions (e.g., grab the tick, pull the tick out) and closing actions (e.g, disinfect the wound, write down the date). Table 1 presents the nine actions and their frequencies in the corpus. The only action that occurs in all MIs is 'pull the tick out'. All actions in the corpus are expressed as processes with an imperative verb. Most MIs ($N = 7$) contain five actions which the user should carry out to perform the task 'neem' (take), 'pak vast' (grab), 'trek uit' (pull out), 'ontsmet' (disinfect) and 'noteer' (write down). Some MIs omit the instruction to take the tweezers (MI8 and MI10), some MIs include other actions, for instance to wash hands after contact with the tick, to take a photograph of the wound, to monitor the victim's health or to visit a GP. In four MIs alternative actions are offered for cases in which a particular action cannot be performed. These cases usually include a conditional. For instance MI18 suggests to grab the head of the tick as near to the skin as possible, if the user has no tweezers at hand, while MI13 instructs the victim to visit a GP if the tick was not removed successfully.

Control information: Control information is included about seven times per MI, usually in the form of warnings and explanations, incidentally also conditionals or motivations occur. Warnings include negated actions like, not to damage the tick (M18), not to drip any liquids on the tick (MI15), or not to crush the tick (M13). Explanations discuss the dangers of a Lyme disease infection or inform the user that it is not harmful if parts of the mouth of the tick are left behind in the skin as a result of pulling the tick out.

2.2 Description of Pictures

The MI pictures were analysed in terms of general characteristics (e.g., type, visualised objects), actions (aspect: process or result) and control information (e.g., warning, explanation, extra information). All MIs in the corpus use five drawn pictures with visualisations similar to the ones presented

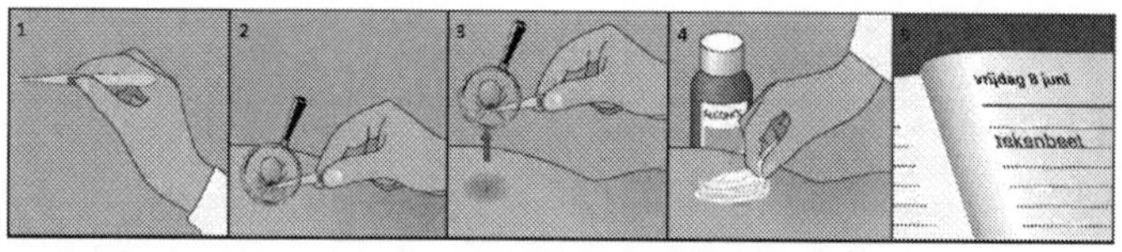

Figure 3: Visualised actions (3,4), and results of actions (1,2,5) in https://thci.nl/teek-pak-beet/.

in Figure 3. These pictures are usually positioned horizontally above or below the instruction. Only in MI13 the pictures are presented vertically to the right of the text. The pictures visualise a number of objects (i.e., tweezers, magnifying glass, tick, wound, flask with alcohol, wipe, agenda, human hands, skin). The magnifying glass is used to show the tick, how to grab it and how to pull it out (see Figure 3). In one MI, MI15 (see Figure 2), an inset in the second picture is used to enlarge the tweezers and the tick as well as to add an exclamation mark to indicate that care should be taken while performing this action. In the picture that visualises the action 'pull the tick out', all MIs use an arrow to indicate the movement as well as the direction in which to pull. The action 'disinfect the wound' is also visualised as a process in which a hand wipes the wound with cotton. However, no arrows appear in any of the pictures to indicate this movement. Not all actions are visualised in the MI pictures as processes. Instead, the result of the action is visualised for the actions: 'pick up tweezers', 'grab the tick' and 'write down the date', where respectively a hand already holds the tweezers, the tick is already grabbed and the date is already noted. Control information in the pictures usually occurs once per MI, in the sense that a magnifying glass is used to provide more detail. The exclamation mark in Figure 2 is an exceptional occurence of a visualised warning.

	Action	Aspect of Action in Text	Number of Verbalised Actions	Aspect of Action in Pictures	Number of Visualised Actions
Preparatory Actions	Pick up the tweezers	Process	9	Result	15
Core Actions	Grab the tick	Process	14	Result	15
	Pull the tick out	Process	15	Process	15
Closing Actions	Desinfect the wound	Process	14	Process	15
	Wash hands	Process	1	-	-
	Write down the date	Process	13	Result	15
	Take a photograph of the wound	Process	1	-	-
	Monitor health	Process	1	-	-
	Visit GP	Process	2	-	-

Table 1: Steps in removing a tick as presented in 15 MIs (control information excluded).

2.3 Text-Picture Relations

Table 1 presents an overview of the actions in the corpus to show how text and pictures are related. For each MI all actions are only counted once; repetitions like the alternative way to pull the tick out without tweezers are not counted. The pictures present the same information in all MIs. In ten cases, the text does not mention an action that is depicted in one of the pictures. Seven of these omissions concern details of the actual pulling-out action: 'pick up the tweezers' (6 cases), 'grab the tick' (1 case). The remaining three omissions concern closing actions: 'disinfect the wound' (1 case), and 'write down the date' (2 cases). Conversely, there are five cases where a verbalised action is not shown in picture. They all concern closing actions, most of which would be hard to visualise in the instruction (e.g. 'monitor health', 'visit GP').

3 User Study

We illustrate the use of text-picture analysis for user-based evaluation of document design with a user study, conducted by the second author as part of her MA thesis research (Eppinga, 2017).

3.1 Setup

The study investigates how horizontal (H) or vertical (V) positioning of the pictures (P) and the text (T) affects the comprehension, recall, performance and attractiveness of a tick-removal instruction. The setup four conditions: HPT ($N = 5$) and HTP ($N = 6$), VPT ($N = 6$), VTP ($N = 6$). The participants in the user study were 22 mothers with at least one child less than 16 years old and with a mean age of 41.2 years. The participants did not hold a first-aid certificate and had no experience with removing ticks. Twelve of the participants worked at the university, including eight in the linguistics department. The education levels of the participants varied, but were balanced across the conditions. Figure 4 displays the four MI versions that were presented to the participants. The MI, with five written instruction steps accompanied by five pictures, presents the basic procedure derived from the results of our corpus analysis. Figure 5 shows the setting in which the participants were recorded on video while reading one of the four MI versions on the screen of an eye tracker and carrying out the instruction using the materials on the tray in front of them: tweezers, cotton, alcohol, pen, agenda, and a puppet with a tick (Figure 6). To avoid ethical issues, the tick was represented by a headed pin located in the armpit of the puppet.

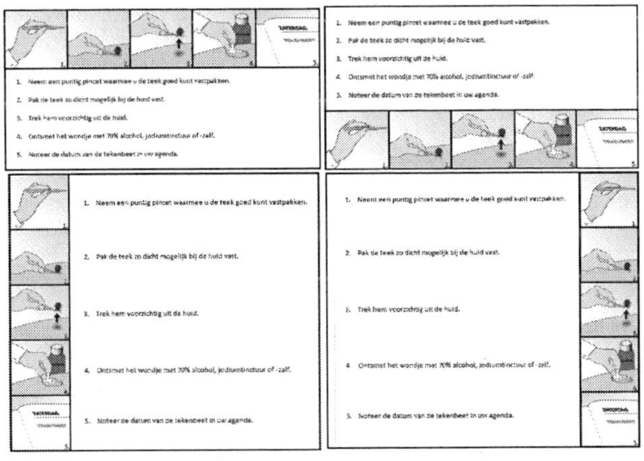

Figure 4: Four versions of the MI to remove a tick f.l.t.r. HPT, HTP, VPT and VTP.

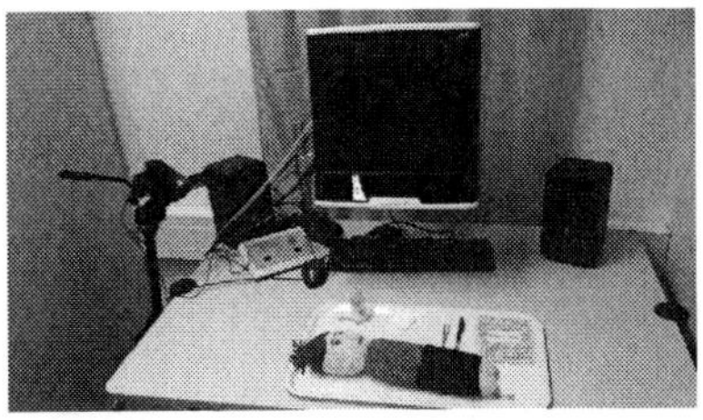

Figure 5: Experiment setting.

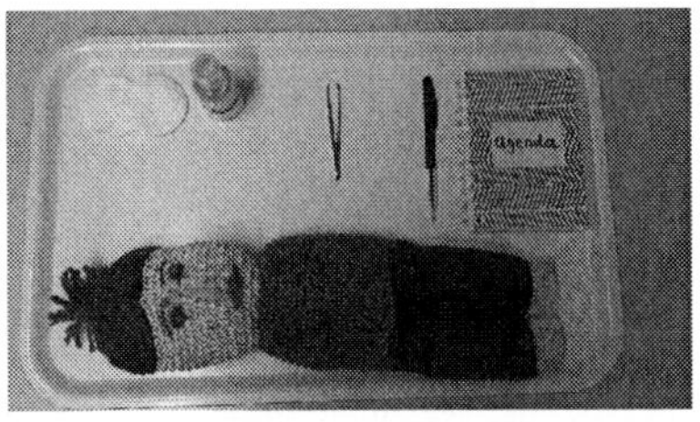

Figure 6: Tick removal materials.

3.2 Procedure

Participants in the study were received in our eye tracking lab and invited to read the introduction to the study. All participants signed a consent form to indicate their voluntary participation and to allow the use of the data they provided for research purposes. Participants first filled out a demographic questionnaire and then sat down in front of the eye tracker and camera. Participants were free to choose their own strategy in carrying out the instruction; in particular, they could switch freely between the screen and the tray. As the researcher was seated out of sight, participants were asked to indicate when they were finished executing the instruction. Once finished, the participants filled out a questionnaire for measuring comprehension and recall. Subsequently, participants were shown all four variations of the instruction and were asked to indicate which one they would prefer to use in real life. Finally, a short semi-structured interview was conducted to gain further insights in the participants experience. The sessions were closed with a debriefing.

3.3 Results

Video analysis and the questionnaires: Table 2 shows that it took participants approximately 70 seconds to process the instruction and carry out the task. No errors were made in the sequence of the instructed actions, however some actions were omitted (1 point) and sometimes the performance quality was suboptimal (0.5 points), or the materials were not properly used (1 point). In total, 2 errors were made in the action 'disinfect the wound' (once omitted and twice suboptimally performed) and 3.5 errors were made in 'write down the date' (twice omitted and three times suboptimally performed), 1 error was due to improper use of attributes. The mean number of switches participants made in looking from the instruction to the task and vice versa, were highest in the conditions HPT and VPT, where the pictures were positioned on the left or above the text. When asked to describe the instruction after finishing it, participants usually recalled four of the five actions. Participants were also able to answer most of the seven cued recall questions correctly and indicated that the MIs were comprehensible. No significant differences were found in these measurements between the conditions. When comparing the four versions of the MI, participants found the vertically oriented designs (VPT and VTP) more attractive than the horizontally oriented ones (HPT and HTP). In the interview participants commented that they considered 'grab the tick' and 'pull it out' as one action instead of two. Moreover, they found the instructions comprehensible and easy to perform, but difficult to recall.

		HPT	HTP	VPT	VTP
Performance	*Duration in seconds*	68.9	71.8	69	71.1
	Total number of errors	0.5	3	2	1
	Number of switches	7.8	5.2	7.8	4.8
Recall	*Free (5 actions)*	4.4	4.6	3.7	4.5
	Cued (7 questions)	4.4	5.2	5.2	5.3
Comprehension	*4 questions*	6.5	6.5	6.7	6.4
Attractiveness (N of choices)	*Most attractive*	4 (18%)	0 (0%)	8 (36%)	10 (45%)
	Least attractive	4 (18%)	16 (72%)	1 (4.5%)	1 (4.5%)

Table 2: User study results (means unless otherwise indicated; comprehension was measured on a scale from $1 = incomprehensible$ to $7 = comprehensible$).

Eye movements: Due to technical issues, the eye tracker data of one participant in condition VTP was discarded. In general participants spent 11.42 seconds reading the text and 2.09 seconds viewing the pictures. Fixation on areas of interest was measured for each verbal step and each picture. In general the text was better studied than the pictures (98.25% versus 80.75%). Interestingly, the picture fixations show that only the pictures in the VTP condition were fully studied (100%), while the pictures in the other conditions drew considerably less attention (HPT= 64%, HTP= 72% and VPT= 87%). All participants started the task execution only after they had fully studied the instruction. The eye tracker data shows that participants always started with reading the first step of the instruction, even when there were pictures placed to the left of or above the text. In the conditions HPT and HTP the pictures were only studied after participants had read the verbal instruction at least as far as step 3. In general, the pictures were studied more thoroughly by the participants in the conditions in which the pictures were placed to the right of or below the text.

4 Conclusion and Discussion

The studies described in this paper present a worked example of annotating and evaluating multimodal content. As the possibilities to describe multimodal content are infinite, we advocate corpus studies and user studies to determine the relevance of annotation categories in situated contexts. Although small scale, results of studies like these allow fine-tuning of annotation models for multimodal content in terms of text, pictures and their relations as implemented in the PAT Workbench (Van der Sluis, Kloppenburg & Redeker, 2016). We are currently developing more fine-grained models that allow specification of functional and content relations between e.g., words, clauses and sentences, and between text and pictures. The application of those models to a wide variety of first-aid instructions (several hundred in our PAT corpus) and their tests in controlled user studies, will inform the development of an evaluation system and design guidelines for MIs.

References

Aouladomar, F. (2005). A semantic analysis of instructional texts. In *Proceedings of the Sixth International Workshop on Computational Semantics (IWCS-6).*

Bateman, J. (2014). Using multimodal corpora for empirical research. In *The Routledge handbook of multimodal analysis*, pp. 238–252. Routledge, London.

Eppinga, A. N. (2017). Van voor naar achter of van links naar rechts? Een onderzoek naar de positionering van tekst en beeld in tekenbeetinstructies. Master's thesis, Communication and Information Sciences, University of Groningen.

Houts, P., C. Doak, L. Doak, and M. Loscalzo (2006). The role of pictures in improving health communication: a review of research on attention, comprehension, recall, and adherence. *Patient Education and Counseling 61*(2), 173–190.

Katz, M., S. Kripalani, and B. Weiss (2006). Use of pictorial aids in medication instructions: a review of the literature. *American Journal of Health-System Pharmacy 63*(23), 2391–7.

Maes, A., A. Arts, and L. Noordman (2004). Reference management in instructive discourse. *Discourse Processes 37*(2), 117–144.

Mayer, R. (2005). *The Cambridge handbook of multimedia learning.* Cambridge University Press.

Schnotz, W. (2005). An integrated model of text and picture comprehension. In *The Cambridge handbook of multimedia learning*, pp. 49–70. New York.

Schnotz, W., I. Wagner, F. Zhao, M. Ullrich, H. Horz, N. McElvany, A. Ohle, and J. Baumert (2017). Development of dynamic usage of strategies for integrating text and picture information in secondary schools. In D. Leutner, J. Fleischer, J. Grünkorn, and E. Klieme (Eds.), *Competence Assessment in Education*, pp. 303–313. Springer International Publishing.

Schriver, K. A. (1997). *Dynamics in document design: Creating text for readers.* Wiley, New York.

Sweller, J. (2016). *Cognitive Load Theory: What We Learn and How We Learn.* Springer International Publishing.

van der Sluis, I., L. Kloppenburg, and G. Redeker (2016). PAT Workbench: Annotation and evaluation of text and pictures in multimodal instructions. In *Proceedings of the Workshop on Language Technology Resources and Tools for Digital Humanities (LT4DH) at COLING 2016*, pp. 131–139.

van der Sluis, I., S. Leito, and G. Redeker (2016). Text-picture relations in cooking instructions. In H. Bunt (Ed.), *Proceedings of the Twelfth Joint ISO - ACL SIGSEM Workshop on Interoperable Semantic Annotation (ISA-12) at LREC 2016*, Volume 16, pp. 22–27.

van Hooijdonk, C. and E. Krahmer (2008). Information modalities for procedural instructions: The influence of text, pictures, and film clips on learning and executing RSI exercises. *IEEE Transactions on Professional Communication 51*(1), 50–62.

AUTHOR INDEX